Rural Reflections

Rural Reflections

by

Isobel Eastman

Canadian Cataloguing in Publication Data

Eastman, Isobel, 1935-
    Rural Reflections

ISBN 0-9687544-0-6

1. Eastman, Isobel, 1935-   -- Childhood and youth
    2. Farm life--Ontario--Lanark (County)--History.
    3. Lanark (Ont.: County)--Biography.   I. Title.

FC3095.L37Z49 2000   630'.92   C00-900932-9
F1059.L3E28 2000

Publisher: Isobel Eastman
              Rural Press
              R.R. #3,
              North Gower, ON
              K0A 2T0

Printed and bound in Canada by Transcontinental Printing.
Cover design and typesetting by Bob Kingham, Ottawa.
Consulting services on publication by Elaine Kenney,
            Communication Matters, Ottawa.

Photos on pages 41 and 70 by Steve Coleman.

Cover photo: From a 1941 newspaper article showing the author (left) with her sister Lois and two of ninety-four chinchillas which arrived at the family farm near Pakenham.

TABLE OF CONTENTS

FOREWORD
by Mary Cook

RURAL REFLECTIONS ARE JUST that and much more as they reflect the memories of Isobel Eastman. They make up a collection of authentic stories of a special era in rural Ontario. The warmth and often the humour, revealed in the stories has the reader anticipating the next journey down Memory Lane.

Storytelling is a lost art, and it is a joy to find a writer who has been able to transport us through her memories, along a delightful road. This is a book for every bookshelf, to share space with other treasured volumes, to be picked up at leisure and to be cherished as a true reflection of what stories from the heart should be.

Mary Cook is a local author and broadcaster/ journalist having been with CBC for 44 years. She has written six books on the depression years and a biography on her mother; Mary is a seven-time ACTRA award winner.

DEDICATION

MY FATHER, WILLIAM THOMAS McGILL, was born in 1886 and died in 1967. His friends called him Tom. His eyes crinkled at the corners from years of working in the sun and from laughter.

I was the youngest of four children and a child of his older years, so I spent much time with him. We talked, we sang, we went to hockey games together, played cribbage and generally hung out together. He whittled willow whistles and taught me songs he loved. Dad was a consummate storyteller and it was from him that I learned this craft. And so, I dedicate these stories to him, to my Dad, who inspired me to remember the stories of my youth and pass them on to the next generations. His tales and his laughter will always live in my memory and in my heart.

A GIANT AMONG MEN

HE WAS NOT BIG in stature, or strikingly handsome, or a great conversationalist. But he was my Dad and he was a giant among men.

Someone once said that the eyes are the windows to the soul. Dad had the bluest, most sparkly eyes you could ever imagine and they served as a window to his soul—the dearest soul that ever walked this earth. His eyes crinkled at the corners from years of working in the sun and from laughter that came easily to him. Perhaps his mischievous, laughing Irish eyes made him ageless. He was one generation removed from the Irish soil and his stories of Ireland intrigued our young ears. Most certainly, the more receptive his audience was, the more he embellished his stories. When you listened to him, you had the impression that he was right there suffering through the horrible days of starvation when field after field of potatoes fell to the dreaded black blight.

He often told the strange story of chance that brought his family to Canada—a story involving poverty, hunger and witchcraft. The witchcraft part added an eerie element to his story. It also formed a unique part of my Dad's heritage.

Our history lessons told of the poverty and hunger surrounding the potato famine in Ireland, and the McGill family suffered from poor crops — as did every other farming family. Should they emigrate to Australia or should they stick it out on their poor run-down farm in Ireland? The difficult decision had to be made.

Grandfather's family was not large by Irish standards; he only had 2 siblings. Although the older ones worked alongside their father in the fields, they had absolutely no say in whether the family should go or remain to fight the potato famine. The parents struggled with the choices. After days of uncertainty, they reached a decision in a most supernatural way.

My Dad's grandfather was trying to squeeze enough milk for the morning's porridge out of their only remaining cow when an old woman suddenly appeared. It seemed as if she came from nowhere! She was haggard and stooped, with sharp features and hollow piercing eyes. She asked for a tin of milk from his meagre supply. Sadly, he refused her, saying he only had enough milk for his family, and none to spare. Pointing her scrawny finger at the cow, she uttered some unintelligible chant, and disappeared as mysteriously as she had come.

From that moment on, his story goes, the cow gave no more milk. Not a drop. They believed that a curse uttered by the old woman/witch caused the cow to go dry.

That did it! The decision then became an easy one. They could not stay in a land where witches roamed the countryside practising their craft. They packed their belongings and said their goodbyes to neighbours. Within a few days they appeared at the dock with all their worldly belongings stuffed in a few dilapidated trunks and crates.

They had received assurance of passage on a ship leaving for Australia, and prepared themselves for a long ocean journey. When the Australian ship was delayed because of heavy seas, the patriarch of the family blamed the old witch for once again interfering in their lives. Anxious to get far away from her powers as quickly as possible, he loaded his wife and children onto a small ship sailing to Canada. My grandfather, my Dad's father, made that ocean journey as the youngest of the family.

Dad used to remark, after telling this tale, that he might have been herding kangaroos instead of Holsteins, but for that old woman and her curse!

The travel-weary Irish emigrants finally settled in Lanark County. The homestead they fashioned from local logs is the same one where both my Dad and I were born.

My Dad attended school until the 5th grade, often sporadically, because they needed him to work on the farm. In spite of this, and because he was an intelligent man, he attained a wealth of general knowledge. He read all the great authors—Dickens, Shakespeare, Keats, Conan Doyle, Service—and many others. I can't recall where we got all the books, but he spent part of every evening with a novel in his hands.

In the winter, he filled the stove with wood and sat with his feet in the oven door until he got cold enough to rouse himself and stoke the fire. I recall coming in late one winter night and finding him engrossed in his latest book, feet in the oven, toque on his head, mitts on his hands, and wearing his winter overcoat. The fire had long since died, but he read on!

As he read, he often smoked cigarettes and ate chocolates—two bad habits married to one good one. We frequently urged him to quit smoking, but he would reply, "Quitting smoking is easy. I've done it several times!" He devised many lame excuses for continuing to smoke and often declared that a man is entitled to at least one vice.

As Dad aged and developed many health problems, we grew even closer. I treasured the time we spent together. During hospital visits I shaved his wrinkled face and endured the teasing about the lack of skill I possessed in this art.

He was a poor patient, not content with hospital confinement or hospital food. Eventually the only food that appealed to him was peas brose—a disgusting muddy-coloured porridge made of ground pea flour. It wasn't in great demand, but the local flour mill carried it and the hospital encouraged us to feed it to him. It was the only treat he enjoyed. At that point, not even chocolates or books interested him any longer.

When he died, I felt the expected grief and loneliness. Even yet, I hear his deep bass voice in the hymns he enjoyed and I hear his laughter ringing in my head when I remember shared jokes.

He often said that the creek you used to jump gets wider as you get older. So it probably was with his stories, but that took nothing away from their entertainment value. I feel as if my children and grandchildren have missed something vital in not knowing my Dad and hearing his stories. He left me with a treasure of warm memories, and many experiences that I try to pass on to the next generation. This book contains many of those recollections of my growing-up years in a rural environment.

For these reasons I dedicate this book to him. For it is he who inspired me to share my memories with you. Perhaps my images of him are a bit larger than life, but this wonderful man left a lasting impression on me. At five foot ten, he was a giant among men.

CHARLIE, THE CHICKENS AND ME

IT WAS WHEN THE backyard chickens skittered furiously that we knew Charlie was coming back.

The dust swirled in all directions as those witless birds ran in circles squawking with fear, wings flapping, their little claw feet moving frantically. Yet they seemed to make no headway in escaping from Charlie. The birds must have heard him before I did, or with some fowl sixth sense felt his approach. I almost felt sorry for those helpless hens when he invaded their private backyard. And I didn't even like chickens!

Charlie, the pilot-in-training, posed no real threat to us as long as he stayed up in the sky where he belonged. But I don't believe he ever knew what fear he instilled in me and those chickens.

What was I doing in the yard to begin with? Well, our yard consisted of packed Lanark County clay that swirled with dust eddies on windy days. Farm machinery continually passed through it, loosening the clay, which resulted in bumps and hollows covered in dust. This meant war for my Mom, and the broom battalion went into action. She felt that our backyard should be swept at least once a week. I never revealed this fact to my friends; it was far too embarrassing, and one thing that set us apart from them.

After many years, I finally realized what she was up to. Sweeping the dust and keeping the backyard neat was just a ploy. She didn't care all that much about a pristine backyard. She simply assigned us "busy work" to occupy our idle hands and minds. When I started to assign busy work to my own children, I finally understood.

The well-swept backyard was enclosed on one side by a chicken pen and on another side by a woodshed. A machine shed completed the third side. The configuration of buildings gave us a pseudo-courtyard, leaving one side open. Charlie attacked from the open side.

On that ill-fated, windy summer afternoon I was in the backyard sweeping. As quickly as I swept, the wind blew away my neat piles of dust. It seemed an exercise in futility. Nevertheless, I continued; after all, it was my appointed task and duty. As I swept, the chickens paraded—no, strutted—around the yard, defying me to swat them. Could it be that fowl sixth sense again? They knew it was trouble for me if I threatened them.

Suddenly they started to squawk and run around wildly! A horrendous thundering sound came from behind me. I ran around in much the same pattern as those birds, with dust flying off my heels.

I had no idea what was happening, but the noise increased and my heart pounded with fear. Then something huge dived straight down, out of the sky, right at me and the chickens. I ducked, letting out a terrified screech, not unlike the chickens' squawks.

It was Charlie! That bold, daring, show-off Charlie. He had just received his pilot's licence and was eager to tell the world. Like an enemy pilot, he attacked, approaching from the open side of our peaceful, well-swept courtyard. His one-seater training plane zoomed down so low I felt I could reach out and touch the propeller. All that was missing was gunfire. As quickly as he appeared, he disappeared over the shed. Like Superman he was up, up and away.

It took the chickens and me half an hour to recover from the surprise attack. My carefully gathered pile of dirt was just a memory; it had swirled back to its original resting place, making a mockery of my diligent labour.

Later that day, Charlie came to brag about the event. He clearly failed to understand our fear. He regarded the "buzzings" as hugely successful capers, but they had a lasting effect on me—I still fear flying!

It came as no surprise that Charlie joined the war as soon as he was old enough to legally enlist. There would be no marching in the infantry for him.

He had tramped after enough cows and horses, just over the hill, on the next farm, to last him a lifetime. Charlie was headed for something with glamour, excitement and speed, so he trained to be a fighter pilot in the Royal Canadian Air Force.

It was this training that became the bane of our existence for the chickens and myself. Charlie continued to inflict the same daredevil display on us again and again. We were never prepared for these dramatic attacks and I lived in dread that on one of his visits, he might not pull up fast enough and would crash into the shed or into us.

But it never happened. Charlie survived the entire war with no serious accidents over our farm or in the European skies. After the war, he settled down to a life of quiet predictability in a nearby small town. But he always drove a flashy car at high speeds!

HIRAM AND FLOSSIE

"WHAT HAPPENED TO YOUR back window, Hiram?" Hiram had just circled into the backyard with his '38 Chevy.

I was out sweeping again, doing busy work, thanks to another of Mother's cleaning fits. Hiram's '38 Chevy, which was used as his farm vehicle, always had hay hanging off it somewhere—out the back door, trailing behind or caught on his bumper. The vehicle had various scratches and dents of unknown origin which added to its general appearance of neglect. But today the back window on the driver's side had a big hole with radiating cracked glass. Some hay was caught in the hole.

"It was Billy," he stated as way of explanation. Hiram wasn't loquacious. You had to be patient, knowing that eventually the whole story would come out. I knew that Billy was Hiram's male goat.

Hiram wasn't all that creative when it came to naming his animals. The old sow was called "Pig," and even though he had owned several teams of horses over the years, they were always called "King" and "Queen," no matter what gender they were. Every bull he ever owned was "Bert." I suppose it made life a little easier for Hiram not having to part with a name when an animal was replaced.

"How'd he manage that?" I asked. Anyone who talked to Hiram immediately fell into the same speech patterns—using as few words as possible.

"Had him in the back seat. He didn't like it."

Those who didn't know Hiram might wonder why Billy the goat had been in the back seat of the only vehicle he owned. I knew the whole story would unfold, but in his time frame. And besides, while I was visiting with Hiram, I didn't have to sweep the yard. So I leaned on my broom, patiently waiting for the details to spill out a bit at a time. I wondered how he could stand the smell of Billy in his Chevy. Goats give off a very powerful odour, and Hiram's animals had a particularly offensive smell about them.

"Is he in the car now?"

"Nope. I dropped him off at Nanny's for a visit." I was only 11 years old, but living on the farm had taught me all the little codes that farmers used to avoid sensitive topics. What Hiram had really said in that cryptic response was quite clear to me. He had left his goat, Billy, at his brother Harvey's place in order to breed Harvey's goat, Nanny. (Harvey and Hiram shared a fondness for simple names.) It was unthinkable to talk about breeding to a young girl, so he adroitly skirted the topic.

Billy's visit could have lasted considerably less than several hours, but Hiram let Billy stay with Nanny that long—just to be sure. And of course, while Billy was taking care of Nanny, it gave Hiram a chance to visit with us.

He often came to visit around 11:30 in the morning. Dinner on the farm was at noon. It wasn't long before Mother called from the back door, greeting Hiram and calling me in to eat.

"Want to come in for dinner, Hiram?" Mother asked.

"Guess I could," replied Hiram. His place was already set at the table. Mother knew that invitations for meals were always accepted.

We loved when he stayed for a meal, because then we got to see his hair. Hiram always wore a peaked hat well over his eyes. He had those Bette Davis kind of eyes that were only half open at the best of times. With his peaked cap pulled over his eyes, we wondered how he ever saw at all.

But it was his hair that sent us into fits of snickering. Mother would warn us with her eyes to behave and refrain from giggling, however, it was very hard for my sister and me. We knew the routine. He would wash his hands in the wash basin and at the very last minute, before he sat down at the table, he would remove his hat. The hat stayed on his head all day, every day, and we suspected that he even wore it to bed. He knew my mother wouldn't let him come to the table with the hat on, so he waited until the very last instant to remove it. When he took off his hat, his shaggy black hair lay flat. Except at the back of his head. Up popped three spikes of unruly hair, and they stood straight up. Just like dandelions rising up after the lawn mower goes over them. We knew these spikes were going to pop up and we waited for them. When they reached their full height, my sister and I started to giggle. Poor Hiram. I wonder if he ever knew what amused us. More eye threats from Mother made us straighten up right away.

A week after Billy's visit to Nanny, Hiram was having dinner with us again. When he took off his hat before dinner, there were no spikes popping up. Instead, his hair was all greased down and slick as a polished stovepipe. We glanced at each other with disappointment, and even Mother took a long look as she passed behind him on her way to the table.

Several weeks later, we learned why. Hiram had a woman in his life. It turned out to be Flossie—Flossie was what my Mother called "a crackerjack" of a nurse, who worked at the local hospital. One day they arrived at our place with Flossie sitting cuddly close to him in the front seat of the Chevy. We thought it was very romantic, but it seemed out of character for Hiram, and we later found out the real reason. Billy had chewed the upholstery on the passenger side of the front seat, and the springs were exposed. Flossie had to sit close to Hiram, if she didn't want a spring poking her in the back end.

Hiram and Flossie were married after a respectable period of courting. Their honeymoon was in Niagara Falls. When they returned, Dad had to pick them up at the train station to take them home. Niagara Falls must have been good for Hiram, because he met my Dad with a big grin and a new look of resolve. Dad shook Hiram's hand and congratulated him on his marriage.

The old bashful look returned. He shuffled his feet on the ground and kept his eyes cast down. Then he replied, "The same to you, Tom!"

This reply made Flossie giggle, and she poked Hiram in the ribs. On the trip home, Flossie continued to giggle at every comment Hiram made to Dad about their trip to Niagara Falls.

We saw less of Hiram for meals after that, except when Flossie was away on a refresher course or when Nanny needed Billy. The neighbours were all curious about how Hiram latched onto a good thing like Flossie, but Hiram was tight-lipped and never told the story of their romance.

During their marriage Flossie was feisty, full of get-up-and-go, and kept Hiram on the move. The house was painted, flowers were planted, and the lawn was cut and kept tidy. And even Hiram was clean and well dressed.

The one thing that never changed was his peaked hat. It was an integral part of him, and Flossie lost the battle to replace it.

Many years later Flossie died suddenly. Hiram once again came to our house for dinner. He washed his hands at the wash basin, took off his hat, and sat at the table. The greased-down hair was gone and the three spikes were back, standing as tall and proud as ever!

BOB, ERNIE AND THE B-B SHOTS

AS BOB LIFTED THE bottle of booze to his lips, Ernie slackened the reins of the horses. That was Ernie's second mistake. The first mistake was trusting Bob with the bottle. The bottle never quite reached Bob's lips.

The country quietness this summer evening was broken only by the clop, clop, clopping sound of the old team of plugs as they travelled down the dirt road towards home. Fortunately, the horses knew the way home, because Bob and Ernie couldn't have found their way out of a backhouse. As was their custom every Saturday, the brothers had spent several hours at the local watering hole, and were headed home to recover.

Once home, they were usually unable to get out of their buggy, so they would spend Saturday night there sound asleep. The well-trained team of horses parked the buggy under the branches of the old oak tree in their yard near their house and waited patiently to be unhitched. Early Sunday strollers would hear the sound of snoring rising from the parked buggy. The Saturday night escapades were common knowledge, so no one disturbed the sleeping boys.

When Bob's wife died, Ernie moved in "to take care of Bob." Their yard was tidy, their lawns well mowed. Like most men "batching it" they only did the bare necessities inside the house. But they always washed the week's dishes every Saturday noon, before heading out to the neighbouring village and their favourite drinking establishment.

On this particular Saturday, as usual, Bob and Ernie had spent the afternoon imbibing. It was just before dusk. The summer day was ending and there was a quietness about the countryside, except for the sound of the horses' hooves and a certain ping! The ping of the dead-on accurate B-B shot!

I was secretly perched in the drive shed loft as the buggy carrying the two inebriated brothers passed our farm. Just as Bob lifted the bottle of whiskey to his mouth—ping! The team of horses bolted and took off at the gallop—well, maybe an accelerated trot. It was age, not booze, that impaired the horses! The buggy carrying Bob and Ernie gave a sudden lurch forward, throwing them both back against the seat. The bottle fell from Bob's grip, landed on the road and smashed into a thousand pieces.

They had no idea what had spooked the horses, nor did they seem to care. It took them a quarter of a mile to right themselves and get the horses under control. They had no more booze, but they were still able to sing. The sound of "Roll Out the Barrel" could be heard as they disappeared from our vantage point in the loft.

Here was how the attack was planned. My brother J.R. and his friend Ken knew that Bob and Ernie passed by our house every Saturday night, in the same plastered condition. The loft was a convenient place to mastermind the attack, as it had a west window facing the road. It also had gaping boards on the north side, and these cracks allowed them to track the approach of the buggy.

J.R. and Ken were both good shots and either one of them could have been the successful marksman in this adventure. But a toss of a penny and the call of "heads" determined that my brother, J.R., would man the weapon. I watched from my hiding place, as J.R. put the B-Bs in the gun and cranked it, ready to fire. He steadied the gun against the window frame and waited for the buggy to come into sight. Ping, ping, echoed the B-B gun as it hit its mark. "Bullseye!" shouted J.R.

J.R. regarded his shot as a bonus. Not only did the B-B hit the horse, causing it to rear up, but it did so at a critical moment—just as the bottle was touching Bob's mouth. The B-B shots were harmless and didn't hurt the horses or the men, but they sure spooked that old team.

As Ken and J.R. were splitting themselves laughing at the success of their prank, they finally noticed that I had witnessed the whole thing. They realized that I would become the significant little pest that might squeal on them. And I would, just as sure as "pussy's a cat!" They were usually very good at teasing and manipulating me for their own ends, and now I had an opportunity to pay them back! After many threats and warnings they let me go free, but I had a powerful tool in my possession—the knowledge of what they had done to Bob and Ernie. Mom and Dad would surely not be pleased to learn of the shooting episode, and punishment might be in store for these two delinquents.

For days after the event, whenever J.R. or Ken asked me to do some menial task for them, I would innocently ask, "Have either of you seen the B-B gun lately?" I was immediately let off the hook.

Much to my dismay, my power trip ended unexpectedly!

Apparently Dad had seen the whole episode from the verandah, and knew exactly what had happened. He let the boys enjoy their secret for a few days. He then confronted them with the facts of the prank and punished them by banishing them to the oat field to pull mustard weeds. It was unbearably hot. The field was dry. The weeds were stubborn, and the boys were dusty, sweaty and tired easily from the work. Whenever they eased up on the job, the ping of a B-B gun could be heard from the barn. I got the feeling that Dad enjoyed the boys' sentence as much as the boys had enjoyed their prank with Bob, Ernie and the B-B shots!

Chickens In My Life

THE PERSON WHO COINED the term "birdbrain" must have had extensive exposure to chickens. Along with Winnie the Pooh, chickens fit the description of an animal "with very little brain." My early encounters with these birds did nothing to endear them to me.

Since we didn't have an incubator like many of our neighbours, our baby chicks arrived by mail in the spring and had to be picked up at the post office. Air holes on top of the long flat boxes also served as peek holes. They peeked out and we peeked in. The postman must have dreaded this time of the year— the cartons were a teeming mass of constant movement and peeps. They were cute all right, that is, as long as they were young, fluffy and harmless. But I knew, even as a young girl, that these sweet little yellow balls of down would grow up to be the bane of my existence.

The chickens stayed in the summer kitchen under a heat lamp until they were old enough to survive on their own in the farmyard. It was my responsibility to see that they always had water in an upside-down bottle contraption that served as their watering hole. The problem with the water bottle apparatus was that there were always one or two mentally challenged chicks that got entangled in it. They weren't smart enough to free themselves, so I had to rescue them with my bare hands! I did not enjoy touching this wet, wiggling mass of down. But in addition to freeing them, I had to contend with all the other chicks that immediately ran over to swarm me and peck at my hands, making the task even more onerous. It was a happy day when they were mature enough to leave the summer kitchen and go to the chicken coop. Of course they never stayed in their assigned coop, but took over the backyard with a cocky sense of ownership peculiar to chickens. So I was never completely free from them.

When walking in their territory, it was important to keep your eyes on the ground. It was even more necessary when you were barefoot! It was during their summer free-range days that they strutted around proclaiming ownership of the whole area and left their "signatures" all over the yard. Being the youngest in our family, with the least seniority, it was my weekly duty to make the yard presentable, by ridding it of the "signatures." The old scrawny broom was put into use and the sweeping began. How I feared that my friends would catch me doing such a ridiculous task. It would be the ultimate humiliation!

Cleaning up the chicken mess was a loathsome task, but it was also my lot to gather the eggs. I swear there were two old cackling hens that hated the sight of me. They knew when I was approaching to collect eggs, so they stayed on their nests. As I reached under their feathery bodies to retrieve the hidden treasure, they pecked at me and squawked loudly. They were absolutely brutal. My hands still bear scars from these hen encounters. Frequently the stupid hens would boycott the straw-lined nests of the henhouse, and lay their eggs willy-nilly not only in the surrounding grass, but in secret hiding places all over the farm. On occasion we would accidentally come across these eggs. Estimated age of the eggs was indicated by the strength of the odour emanating from them as we threw them against the barn for target practice. This activity took place on the side of the barn removed from the house. Such reckless and wanton waste of our time would be regarded as frivolous by our elders.

My best friend and next-door neighbour taught me a get-even trick to use on these birds. Finally, sweet revenge! Too much time was spent in my pre-teen years in contact or involvement with hens that I detested! The henhouse at their farm was far enough from their house that we were in no danger of being caught by adults during our clandestine activities. It was the perfect place to exact revenge on these witless birds! We held a hen tightly in a squat position and with one finger drew a line in the dirt in front of the chicken's beak. We drew the line over and over until the bird was hypnotized. When the hen was staring blankly, we cautiously let it go—the bird stayed in one spot for many seconds. We had contests to see whose hen would stay hypnotized for the longest time. During those few seconds these inane birds were completely under our control. Then with a toss of their heads, and blinking of their eyes, the birds would regain their senses—what little they had—and would wander around in a stunned state for several minutes. When they started poking their heads in and out like chickens do, we knew that the spell had worn off and they were back to normal

The prank didn't harm the hens, and it gave me a great deal of satisfaction. This was my revenge on those witless birds. To this day, some 50 years later, the only good chicken as far as I'm concerned is one under a pile of dumplings or on top of bacon in a club sandwich!

SIBLINGS

I WAS GULLIBLE, INNOCENT, the youngest of four, and an easy prey to flattery. Praise me up a bit and I'd do anything.

Take the crab apple fights.

A white picket fence bordered our front lawn on three sides. An old twisted crab apple tree drooped over the fence at one end. It was a perfect tree to climb, but it served other purposes. It was a hiding place when I was needed to do dishes, a pouting place when I was moody, and a secret reading place when I felt pensive.

Most important, it served as an ammunition source for the dreaded crab apple fights!

My brothers' friends would gather by the tree and divide themselves into teams. I was completely flattered when they often chose me first. Next on the agenda was to collect the fallen crab apples from the lawn. We would shake the old, crooked crab tree to release the stubborn fruit clinging to its branches. The ammunition was placed in old honey tins.

One team hunkered down behind the tree by the adjoining fence, while the opposing team mustered around the corner of the house, about 80 feet away. At a given signal, the battle began. Crab apples flew through the air at great velocity. Since some of the apples were rotten, brown and soft, it was an added bonus to splatter the enemy. My job was to keep the supply of apples replenished, so when the honey pail was almost empty, my team shoved me out into the open battlefield amidst the enemy barrage, where I was assigned to fill the pail with the apples that had landed in no-man's territory.

The opposition pelted me with the hard bullet-like crabs. They showed no respect for my gender or young age, but kept up the attack unmercifully. I carried out my duty unflinching! All I needed was praise and a sense of importance, and I would give everything to my battalion. I would replenish the pail, and once again I'd be shoved out into the battlefield. At least that's how I recall it.

The football games were carried out in a similar fashion on the same lawn. Two teams were chosen, but this time I was a liability, not an asset, and so I was always chosen last. After several games, one of my brothers had a brilliant idea. Maybe I could be useful after all. My new job was to run over to the opposing team and hang on to the pant legs of one of the players. Finally, I had become an effective team member! At least, that's how I recall it.

My siblings were masters of manipulation and I was their favourite target. On Saturday nights my brothers went out "girling." The same evening they would tell me what a great little sister I was. In reality, they were again setting me up. They ruffled my curly hair affectionately and told me how cute I was. They declared that their shoes were always the best polished ones, and it was because I did such a good job. I was ready to do anything for them. I had fallen for flattery once again. As a result, I spent much of my time polishing their shoes, trying to live up to my reputation. It took me many Saturday nights to see through their game. At least that's how I recall it.

You would think that by night-time, the torment would end, but it didn't. The bedtime routine for my sister and me consisted of a tuck-in time and goodnight kiss from our Mom. She turned off our lamp and closed the bedroom door. Just above the door frame there was a space where the hall light shone through. Mom would wiggle her fingers in that space, making the light flicker like dancing shadows. It was a lovely, comforting routine. But my sister tried to take advantage of the situation and my gullible nature. After Mom had finished creating the dancing shadows and returned downstairs, my sister would start the scare tactics.

"Look above the door!" she whispered mysteriously. "See the ghost there? Look! There's another one over by the window." I saw whatever she invented. The ghostly conversation continued until I buried my head under the pillow and dissolved into tears. To add to the torture, I was warned not to call Mom, or I'd have to sleep alone. She actually convinced me that sleeping alone would be a worse fate!

My sister also seemed to know a great deal about Hell. She gave graphic descriptions of it and told me that was where I was headed, if I didn't improve my behaviour. It never occurred to me to question her authority. It was at this stage that I would run to Mom. "Will I really go to Hell?" It took much reassurance from her that God still loved me, and that I was not destined for Hell. Strangely enough, my sister was always sound asleep when I returned to our room. At least, that's how I recall it.

My siblings probably were no different from those in any other family, perhaps merely more creative in their manipulation. Begrudgingly, I thank them for those years of "character development." Because of them, I am a mature and feisty adult. But I still detest polishing any kind of shoes, and I am still scared of going to Hell.

DISCLAIMER: In order to protect myself from ensuing lawsuits from my siblings, I offer this disclaimer. The incidents that I have disclosed are true to the best of my knowledge, but they have been recounted from my perspective. They are not meant to discredit any or all of my siblings, whom I respect and love dearly. I have no wish to be removed from the family tree as a result of these disclosures, and I assume I will continue to be included in Christmas celebrations and family reunions. If, perhaps, any or all of you, my siblings, have willed me large sums of money, be assured that I forgive you for your past transgressions and happily accept your gracious benefaction. If, on the other hand, any or all of you have not willed me large sums of money, remember I have total recall of several other stories begging for ink!

MORE OF HIRAM AND FLOSSIE

TIMES HAD BEEN KIND to Hiram and Flossie, and they prospered. The old '38 Chevy was replaced by a half-ton truck of newer vintage. Billy the goat now rode in the back of the truck, usually in quiet dignity. If he was having a frisky day, Flossie rode in the back with Billy, with her arms wrapped around his neck.

Everyone remarked on how well Flossie had made the transition from town life to life on the farm with Hiram. She was often at his side as they repaired fences that had been neglected for many years. They sat close together as they proudly drove around in their half-ton. Hiram usually had a contented look about him, much like Billy after a visit to Nanny. His hair was always slicked down and his overalls were patched and clean. Hiram wore a slightly fancier style of hat now, rather than the old greasy peaked hat that had held flat the three wisps of hair in the days preceding Flossie.

Before long the house had new siding on it and flower gardens appeared in the front yard. In spite of this apparent order and tidiness, there was just one inconsistency. Hiram and Flossie allowed their chickens, geese and rabbits to range freely around their yard. Driving into their place was a downright hazard. Their animals skittered everywhere and were unafraid of visitors. They ran towards a vehicle, not away from it. Stepping out of the car and into their yard was an even greater hazard—animal droppings were everywhere. It was unwise to raise your eyes until you reached the house. As visitors arrived they had to gingerly step around the ubiquitous piles of animal droppings. From my vantage point, a tree just outside their gate, they appeared to be doing some kind of strange dance—their bodies gyrated and spun in all directions to avoid the droppings. What a sight!

Flossie continued to work at the local hospital and was always in great demand to do special nursing. She was capable and compassionate, but had a no-nonsense attitude towards certain types of patients: she scoffed at those who she believed were indulging in self-pity and was particularly hard on pregnant women who had morning sickness.

As my Mother would say, "It's a long road that has no turning." That saying proved true for Flossie. She became pregnant and suffered from severe morning sickness. For the first three months she was sick every day and was the worst possible patient! Hiram seemed to come for visits more frequently during this period, usually at mealtime. Pregnancy was a topic that was never discussed in mixed company, so not a word was said about Flossie, and her condition was never formally acknowledged. At that time, a woman in the family way was not even supposed to be seen in public. But unwritten rules were an abomination to Flossie. As soon as she felt well again, she was out driving around with Hiram in the half-ton and even helping with the tractor work.

One morning several months later, at breakfast time, Hiram drove into the yard. He didn't usually appear that early in the day. He was alone, and seemed happy to accept an invitation to have breakfast with us. He carried on the usual conversation with the men about crops, animals and weather. When the meal was finished and the men were returning to work, Hiram got his hat. He rubbed his fingers through his hair and he looked down at his feet, making little shuffling movements with his boots. He seemed to be trying to tell us something. Finally he summoned enough courage and blurted out, "Flossie got us a baby!"

We were all happy and relieved. We were also eager to know the size and gender of the new arrival.

"That's wonderful, Hiram," said my mother. "Is Flossie all right?"

"Guess so," was Hiram's cryptic reply.

"How much did the baby weigh?" asked my Mom.

"Don't rightly know," Hiram answered.

"Was it a boy or a girl?"

"Must be a girl," Hiram said. "Flossie called her Jane. That's all I know. I didn't check her out!"

My Dad reached over, shook Hiram's hand and said, "Congratulations, Hiram."

Hiram continued looking at the floor and was obviously quite flustered by all this attention. He shyly replied, "Thanks, Tom. The same to you!"

That reply sent my sister and me into a giggling fit. But Mother had perfected the technique of sending eye messages. The one she sent now ordered us to leave the room quickly!

Poor Hiram. Since his wedding, he had never been in a position to receive congratulations and didn't know how to handle this situation. He quickly left, but we noticed a little spring to his step as he walked to his half-ton.

Little Jane proved to be a dear, wee girl and was soon riding in the half-ton with her parents. Flossie often came to visit and, in spite of Mom's disapproval, she nursed the baby in the kitchen in full view of everyone. There were a great many "tsk, tsks" from my prim and proper mother, but Flossie and the baby were always welcome. Perhaps my Mom secretly admired Flossie's ability to flaunt convention.

Flossy was always feisty and determined, and as the years passed she managed to straighten out Hiram, as well as many of the locals. Jane grew up to be the joy of their lives. They worked hard on their small farm to pay for Jane's education and were justifiably proud of her when she graduated with a nursing degree.

The time came for retirement and Hiram and Flossie had a sale in preparation for their move into the village. My father went to the sale like many good neighbours and was surprised to see our three-furrow plough being sold by Hiram. He had borrowed it quite a while back and had neglected to return it.

"Forgot it was yours, Tom," he told my Dad. By the time several other neighbours had reclaimed their borrowed articles, Hiram's sale was considerably smaller!

When Flossie and Hiram left the farming community to live in the village, the neighbours had a farewell party for them and presented them with a new set of dishes. They appeared grateful and pleased that the community had remembered them in such a kindly fashion. For two months things went well— both adjusted to town life.

What happened next, we could never explain. One day the set of dishes was returned – well used and with food still clinging to the plates. It was thought that someone in the neighbourhood must have offended feisty Flossie and poor old Hiram and they wanted no part of the community or the dishes. That little falling-out lasted a year or so and then things returned to normal. They continued to drop in for the occasional visit and a meal. The returned set of dirty dishes was never mentioned!

A Bad Day

IT HAD BEEN A "BAD DAY." I could tell because Mother's forehead was a mass of wrinkles and her eyes were squinted narrow and almost shut. That only happened on "bad days." I was nine years old at the time, but smart enough to make myself scarce when she was in such a state. From experience I knew that I had often contributed to the cause of those "bad days."

I disappeared into the crab apple tree to escape any further reprimands. It was a good place to go. I was out of sight, but still within earshot of any heated adult conversations. For occasions such as this, I always kept a book hidden in the big squirrel hole in the trunk of the crab tree. The attics and the apple tree were my private reflecting places and my refuge when trouble loomed!

I went over the events of the morning and tried to remember if I was responsible for my mother's wrinkled brow. Nothing too drastic came to mind, unless of course she was still upset about the churn. I had helped her clean up and had hung the milk-soaked towels on the clothes line with the rest of the laundry. She knew it was a tough job for me—I was barely tall enough to reach the clothes line.

The churn would never have upset if the phone hadn't rung. But someone had to answer it and mother was busy at the time putting milk into the churn to make butter. I was just trying to be helpful by answering it—after all it might have been someone asking me over to play. I couldn't help it if my skirt caught on the churn handle and tipped the whole thing over before you could say "Jack Robinson."

Mother didn't get angry very often, but at that moment she did! She kept mumbling something about the Minister and spilt milk. I had no idea what he had to do with the situation. I soon found out. He appeared at the doorway as we were on our hands and knees wiping up the mess and made some comment about "crying over spilt milk." Well that did it! Mother's face turned beet red and her forehead started to get those wrinkles again. I don't know what the fuss was all about, after all, he simply had some papers to drop off. He didn't stay long and made a hasty retreat.

Mother wasn't very talkative as we continued to clean up the mess. Then Dad appeared at the door and wondered what we were doing. Mother didn't say a word. As he leaned on the door frame, he announced that he had just backed the truck into the clothes line and knocked it down. He also made a hasty retreat. I decided to follow him.

Things seemed alright at lunchtime, although there wasn't the usual chatter back and forth. I guess Mother was rather tired from the churn adventure and having to do the laundry all over again.

It was that afternoon that I knew things weren't as they should be. She was singing and we knew that she only sang when she was under stress. Actually, we were grateful for that, because as Dad said, "she couldn't carry a tune in a bucket."

She attacked those biscuits with a ferocious determination as she rolled and rolled and rolled until the dough lay quite flat. And as she rolled, she sang "Carry Me Back to Old Virginny," her idea of a good biscuit rolling song. I recognized it from the words, but not from the tune!

I didn't think much about the biscuits until about an hour later when I heard her blurt out "Holy Moses" at the top of her lungs. Something really bad must have happened because "Holy Moses" were the toughest curse words Mother was known to use. I cautiously ventured into the kitchen to see what had caused this outburst. She was looking into the oven at two dozen of the blackest little tea biscuits you ever saw. With a determined step and clenched teeth she flung the whole pan of little black balls out in the backyard for the dogs to eat. The dogs wouldn't touch them!

This was when I disappeared up into the crab apple tree. I had just finished two chapters of *Pollyanna* and was starting the third, when my sister climbed up beside me. With two people, it was a tight fit—it was really a one-person tree. I didn't growl at her this time because she also seemed to need a place of refuge. As she climbed up she said, "Mother's having a bad day."

"I know," I replied. "I think it's because of the churn."

"I thought it was because of the feathers," my sister said.

She explained. She and her friend from next door had been playing on the feather tick mattress in our bedroom. This was a great past time, especially on laundry days when the sheets were off the bed and the feather mattress was fully exposed. Her friend would jump face down on the mattress at the bottom of the bed, squeezing all the feathers to the other end. My sister would then jump on the mattress at the head of the bed, sending all the feathers back to their original spot. But as she jumped, a hole had burst open and feathers flew out all over the place. They had tried to squeeze the feathers back in, but Mother had caught them in the act. The friend very quickly left for home. As Mother sewed up the hole, she once more started to sing! That's when my sister joined me in the tree.

As I picked some of the grey feathers from my sister's hair, we discussed the events of the day and decided that perhaps this was a good time to go to the creek and catch bullfrogs. We agreed that Mother needed time to herself. There was no question in our young minds that it had been a "bad day" for her!

THE ATTICS

AN ATTIC IS A place to store old trunks full of memories, along with out-of-date furniture and clothing. In mystery novels, ladders or squeaky stairs always lead to this forgotten room where a trap door has to be pushed open to gain access.

We were lucky to have two attics. One was above the drive shed where old trunks contained treasures from our rich city aunt—huge sparkly hat pins and jewelled combs. The other, less romantic one, was above the woodshed.

To access the clandestine refuge above the woodshed, you had to pick your way through blocks of wood and old discarded pieces of lumber, finally reaching the ladder leading to the attic. Its clear lack of accessibility made it my favourite. There were no comforts to be found here, only stacks of chicken crates and empty boxes covered with pigeon feathers. This was my thinking place, my dreaming place, my magic carpet that transported me away from the ordinary life on a Lanark County farm.

This was also the only safe place to read forbidden novels. I covered one of the chicken crates with a discarded horse blanket and placed it in front of the window. It became my reading room. One day I heard a noise below me in the woodshed.

I quickly tried to hide my book, but in vain. Part of it, I knew, was still visible. The footsteps were now on the ladder and getting closer. I worked at appearing nonchalant, but my heart was racing with fear. Sweet relief! The footsteps belonged to my sister, who appeared at the top of the ladder. I knew I could out-manoeuvre her and keep the illicit novel secret.

She asked me why I was hiding up in the attic. My reply came quickly. I was always prepared for such a moment. I told my sister that the cat had had kittens and she had moved them to the attic, where I had found them. She was no animal lover and had little interest in cats or kittens. That story seemed to satisfy her, but she wasn't leaving. Not only did she stay, but she looked around the attic nervously, her eyes darting here and there, even to the secret hiding place!

My heart pounded furiously. I was certain she could see the pulsing through my sweater. It was time to make my move, so I pushed her aside and started to leave the attic. It worked. She followed me down the ladder and out of the shed.

It wasn't wise to return to the loft and the clandestine reading right away, so I contented myself with another forbidden activity. The attic lookout above the drive shed was going to see some action.

I suspected it because I had become very adept at "breaking the code." For example, when Dad said, "I won't be needing any help in the barn this afternoon," that really meant he was going to breed a cow, and my sister and I were not to go to the barn. Mom would make sure we stayed away.

Today Dad had asked where the bullets were for the gun. That in itself was not a clue because they often went out shooting ground-hogs. But this time the phrase was accompanied by, "You better go to town and get me some more binder twine." I knew something was up. If this was combined with the slightest nod of his head, it meant that they were going to kill one of the old horses for fox meat. And he certainly didn't want me there to observe the kill.

No one knew that there was a secret lookout where I could watch the whole event—in the drive-shed attic. I had never watched them shoot a horse before; I had simply lacked the courage. But today I felt inquisitive and I knew where to find a ringside seat. There was a small knothole in the drive-shed attic above the pig pen and it overlooked the barnyard where the grisly deed would take place. I brought along some Kleenex tissues, just in case I cried.

"Girls, girls! Where are you?'" It was Mother calling.

"Come on, we have to get the binder twine for Dad." She called for a while, but finally gave up the search, while I hid in silence in the attic.

The men appeared in the yard below. They put a blinder over the horse's eyes. It happened quickly. The shot came and the horse fell. At least I assumed that the horse fell. I really didn't know for sure, because my eyes were squeezed tightly shut and my head was turned away at the sound of the gun. When I finally mustered up enough courage to look through the peephole, there was nothing to see! The knothole was too small to get a panoramic view. The only visible movement was that of the man moving away with the gun. I had a funny feeling in my stomach and suddenly regretted being there. Even though I knew the horse meat was needed for the foxes, shooting the horse seemed so final.

I dashed down the ladder from the attic and returned to my other hide-out in the woodshed attic. It was the best place to go to reflect. It was soothing to be up in the semi-dark secret spot surrounded by chicken crates and boxes. Here I could collect my thoughts. I rooted out of its hiding place my secret naughty book, *Forever Amber*. If my parents knew about it I would be in serious trouble. *Forever Amber* was a steamy sexy story that mentioned body parts I didn't even know I had. I tried to settle down and read, but I had a feeling that I wasn't alone.

And I wasn't! A rustling sound came from behind the crates. Quietly, I crawled towards the noise and stretched to full height to peek over the stacked-up crates. I screamed! A face was looking right back at me. We both screamed. It was my sister. We put our hands over our mouths to muffle the noise. Neither of us wanted any adults finding us here. When the dust settled we laughed silently. Fellow conspirators we were. She informed me that she sneaked up here regularly to read her forbidden sexy book, *Kitty*. It was just by chance that we had never encountered each other before.

We decided not to squeal on each other. We spit, and stamped on it, so it was a real, for-true kind of pact. Just about as good as swearing on the Bible. We considered swearing on *Kitty* or *Forever Amber*, but decided that God would surely punish us if we did. We promised to exchange books. Our secret hiding place was secure.

PIGGYBACK

JENNY SHOULD HAVE KNOWN better. The term piggyback didn't mean that you could ride on the back of a pig. Pigs were not made for that kind of activity—at least the pigs on our farm weren't. They were fat, well-fed porkers with broad backs and minds of their own. They had their own shed where they slept away the better part of each day.

Susie, the big old sow, was the only pig that seemed to object to Jenny's presence.

Now, Jenny had never thought of fraternizing with a full-sized mother pig. That kind of activity was as foreign to her as riding on a streetcar was to us! She was city through and through. She came to our place for a few weeks' holidays one summer in 1946. City life apparently had little to offer a busy 11-year-old girl and we were glad of the distraction, and the extra hands to help with the endless jobs on the farm. Years later, reading Tom Sawyer's "painting the fence" episode made me smile to myself. Tom, my sister and I were soul-mates. We used those same Tom Sawyer techniques on Jenny to con her into the least desirable farm chores. And we had thought we were the inventors of the scheme, not Mark Twain.

We convinced Jenny that feeding the chickens and gathering the eggs was so much fun that we were reluctant to share those wonderful experiences. And it worked! She coaxed us; she pleaded with us for an entire day to let her in on the fun. We finally gave in. We "allowed" her to feed the chickens and search for eggs. The funny thing about it is that the poor, innocent girl actually enjoyed these tasks. It was important that our parents didn't find out about our little manipulation, so we warned Jenny not to let anyone know that she was doing the chicken chores. We informed her that she would be in trouble because our parents were very fussy about the care we gave the chickens and they might feel that a city girl just wasn't up to the job. That did it. She loved being part of a conspiracy and worked away at the chicken chores for the remainder of her stay.

She liked chickens—I didn't. I liked pigs—she didn't! Susie the sow was a quiet old girl who loved having her back rubbed, and she was reasonably tame. She minded her own business and allowed us to go in and out of her pig pen. She virtually ignored us. However, when Jenny was with us, Susie became agitated. Whenever Jenny moved into the pig pen, Susie kept one beady little eye focused on her as if she didn't trust the new face. The fact that Susie was expecting a litter in a few weeks probably made her a bit anxious even without Jenny's presence.

At the end of two weeks, Jenny's family came to pick her up and return her to civilization in the city. We were really sorry that Jenny was leaving—sorry for several reasons. Most important, we were going to lose our slave labourer. She had taken her job seriously as chicken caretaker, egg gatherer and car washer. She had even assisted in the hated sweep-the-yard routine. We were just beginning to convince her what fun it was to work with the pigs. This was a more difficult task, because to city folk, pigs have a repulsive odour. She was having difficulty getting past the smell part and seeing the hogs as potential friends. Unfortunately this part of our plan needed some fine tuning, as she just wasn't taking to the pigs the way we had anticipated. The arrival of Jenny's family meant that we would once again be forced to resume all the menial tasks we had convinced Jenny were such fun. It had been a great holiday for us. Our city cousin genuinely enjoyed being the hero in mastering the difficult tasks we had conned her into doing. Our rationale was that both parties had benefited.

When we gave her sister Martha a tour of the farm, Jenny was showing off all that she had learned during her short stay. My sister and I were really proud of our student and encouraged her at every opportunity to exhibit her skills related to farm chores. She basked in the limelight and enjoyed the praise being heaped on her. When we approached the pig pen, her sister suggested that we skip this area— she wasn't enamoured with the pungent pig odour! However, Jenny was determined to prove herself capable in all areas, even with the pigs. She insisted on dealing with Susie.

She entered the pig pen while we watched from the entrance. There was no door—just a low opening that was big enough for pigs. People had to duck to enter. It was about four feet high—not high enough for what happened next.

Jenny was "on a roll" and was trying to impress us all, so she sauntered confidently over to Susie the pregnant pig. Susie stayed still, but had fire in her beady little eyes. That was enough to scare both my sister and me. We called to Jenny to come along and leave Susie alone, but she insisted on staying. She then did something that shocked us and that she would regret soon enough. In an effort to prove herself as really being countryfied, she climbed on Susie's back and tried to ride her around the pen. This was not part of Susie's agenda. She objected and bolted for the door, the door that was only high enough for a pig. Susie dashed out the opening and headed for the barnyard and freedom.

Jenny was knocked out cold after she slammed into the top of the door frame. Her poor sister almost passed out too when she saw Jenny lying apparently lifeless on the ground. Panic took control for a few minutes, but some cold water from the nearby pump revived them both fairly quickly. We were terrified about what our parents would say. We would be blamed, because visitors were always blameless.

Jenny was very noble about the whole event. In spite of the big goose egg on her head and the barnyard dirt her clothes, she assigned no blame to my sister or me. She tried to convince the adults that nothing much had happened, but her efforts were in vain. Mom and Dad quickly pieced together the event and were most apologetic to the city folk. My sister and I were held responsible and duly punished. It was two summers before Jenny returned to the farm for holidays. And when she did, she took care to stay clear of the pig pen!

TOMBOY

PERHAPS THE TOMBOY SCENE would never have happened if I had indulged more often in thought before action. But I seldom did. I reacted first and thought about it after. As a result, I often found myself in precarious predicaments.

In my life, it never rained—it was a deluge. I embellished most conversations with exaggerated gestures. This emotive manner extended into all areas of my early adolescence. As a 13-year-old with raging hormones and undeniable mood swings, I was the stereotypical teenager—rash, abrasive and headstrong. I had what you would call an overactive sense of the dramatic.

I was the only one in the class to write with a backhand script; the rest produced the standard legible cursive writing. I sang loudly and dramatically with accompanying tosses of my head at the appropriate times. I dreamed in Technicolor, and was always the heroine of my romantic fantasies. It was this character flaw, this sense of the dramatic, that often got me into trouble.

The day of the Tomboy disaster started off much like all the other days in my 13th year. Every morning, for me, the first thing to deal with was the dilemma of adopting a particular persona. This was always a challenge! How dull life must be for those who exist with only a solitary persona. I felt blessed to have so many available options—Cutie Pie, Miss Delicate, Joker or Tomboy. Finally I chose. Today would be a Tomboy day! Once that decision was made, preparations for school fell into place as if I were on automatic pilot. Jeans, loose shirt, socks and runners almost jumped out of the closet, knowing that it was their turn today! Wrinkles didn't matter with Tomboy, so ironing wasn't necessary. Time was not wasted on hairstyle. My unruly curls were flattened under a cap, and the cap was turned backwards.

The Tomboy routine demanded that I swagger, with slouching shoulders and hands in my jean pockets. This was going to be one beauty of a day! I didn't merely sit down on the chair for breakfast; I straddled the seat, facing the back of the chair, and waited for someone to notice the look of the day. No one did. How did it happen that I was born into such a boring bunch?

The Tomboy days were the most invigorating ones. I left for school on my bike—riding like a jock, with head bent over the handlebars and knees pumping furiously.

Everything went as expected in the morning. As I entered the classroom, the teacher looked at me with raised eyebrows, and uttered a faint sigh. There could be trouble ahead. Mrs. Sanders knew where Tomboy's actions could lead.

Class proceeded with the usual warnings from the teacher to settle down and "focus." It was very difficult to concentrate on dangling participles when I was so energized. Surely life had more to offer than searching through meaningless paragraphs for words that hung on. When I auditioned for a Hollywood movie no one was going to ask how I felt about dangling participles.

Finally it was noon hour. If only I had taken my seat like everyone else, eaten lunch, chatted, and then gone to the washroom, it might not have happened. But Tomboys don't sit passively. They engage in events around them.

I straddled the chair and started lunch. Bert sat down beside me. He usually did when I was Tomboy. But then Bert was an understanding friend and accepted me in whatever role I played.

The broken chair was what started it. Bert's chair seemed a little wobbly, and on closer inspection we discovered that three of the four rungs had sprung out of place. Bert was ready to get another chair, but that didn't suit me! I flipped his chair upside down over my knees. I did it in true Tomboy fashion, with a flair that caused people to look my way. Success at last; I was being noticed!

I insisted that I could fix those "little sprung suckers." The furnace room was just down the hall, and I quickly returned with a hammer. I grabbed the chair and held onto the inverted legs as if I knew what I was doing. One bang with the hammer on one sprung rung and it sank into place.

Across the room, Sarah Hedley heard the noise. Sarah—tall, with long flowing straight blonde hair— she was Miss Perfect.

Sarah stood up and berated me for my well-intentioned repair efforts in a phony, syrupy kind of voice. "For heaven's sake. Must you make so much noise?"

It was, of course, a question that didn't require an answer, but I couldn't let it go. Up to this point, the day had been all that I could hope for. That one snide comment started the deluge.

As Miss Perfect was about to resume her seat and proceed with being flawless, my Tomboy persona felt a surge of energy and focused on Miss Perfect. It seems like things then happened in slow motion—it was like Neil Armstrong taking those first steps on the moon surface—slow, bouncing motions, but purposeful. I clutched the hammer in my right hand and raised it above my head. Like a pitcher going through the windup, my left foot lifted off the floor. The hammer hand went back. I aimed at the unsuspecting Miss Perfect with a threatening motion.

Then the unexpected happened. It was only meant to be a threat—nothing more, but at that moment the whole game plan disintegrated into chaos. The 10-ounce steel head of the hammer flew off and tumbled through the air, rolling end over end. It was a ridiculous thought, but it resembled the way the numbered balls tumbled in the big clear Bingo Ball.

Miss Perfect laughed as she talked to the girl beside her, unaware of the missile flying in her direction. The 10-ounce steel hammer head missed her perfectly groomed head by inches, sailed by her ears and crashed through the window. It fell harmlessly into a bed of geraniums just outside the window. Miss Perfect paled with fear as she realized what had almost happened. I turned a deep shade of guilt-ridden red as I considered the near hit. When would I ever learn? Yes, I received the attention all right, but not in the manner I had hoped for. Even Bert deserted me and hovered with concern over Miss Perfect.

It was another case of reacting before thinking. At first, I felt that paying for the window repair and a three-week detention was unfair punishment. After all, the hammer head fell off by accident, and it actually hadn't hit anyone, just the geraniums.

I accepted the punishment, and the responsibility, and used the time to consider the error of my ways. I also spent a considerable amount of time skilfully preparing my next persona. I would out-perfect Miss Perfect! After all, I had the gift of three whole weeks to work on the plan!

THAT @#$^&%$ HORSE

"@#$^&%$" UNCLE JAKE CURSED a lot when he was angry. He must have been angry often, because the strongest memories I have are of Uncle Jake cursing.

He looked like Santa Claus with blue bib overalls. And like Santa, he had a moustache and two red cherry spots on his cheeks that expanded to tomato size when he was angry. His pin-sized eyes could open as widely and quickly as a camera lens, depending again on his mood. One of his shoulders was lower than the other, making the wide strap on that side of his overalls droop uselessly over his arm. Every minute or so he had to hitch up the strap.

A pipe always dangled from his mouth and he constantly chewed on it. Sometimes he even lit it. He often chewed tobacco and had developed the art of spitting tobacco to an expert level. An old brass spittoon rested on the floor near his big bay window, where he sat on a huge window seat. It was large enough to hold six kids, but Uncle Jake could barely fit on it. When he lay there, he reminded me of Gulliver, in *Gulliver's Travels*—he was that big. From his position on the window seat, he took a glance at the spittoon, aimed, and let fire with a ball of brownish tobacco juice. What a shot he was! We would hover around him, waiting to see if he would miss the spittoon. But he never did. We were often tempted to move the brass spittoon, but our fear of him far outstripped our mischievousness.

"That @#$^&%$ horse!" That's what we heard when we drove past Uncle Jake's farm one day. His high-pitched curse words were garbled by both the speed of his speech and his floppy moustache. We could barely understand a word he was saying.

The curse words reached us through the open windows of our half-ton. It didn't bother me, because this was old stuff to me, but my passenger had never heard anything like it. B.J. was a city girl and was visiting the farm for the first time. I had hoped to charm her with a quiet, pastoral scene of cows and horses grazing peacefully—no such luck!

As we approached the farm, we saw the lifeless arms of Uncle Jake's windmill. A working windmill, it was used to pump water for his livestock. There was always a breeze at the top of his hill and the windmill arms usually pushed gently through the air, moving the pump handle up and down to fill the trough with water. Today, the windmill arms remained still, and the hill was full with neighbours' trucks. As we drew closer we noted a big crane perched close to the well under the windmill.

"@#$^&%$." This was really embarrassing. My friend B.J. and I had met at a church camp, and this kind of language wasn't what she was used to.

"@#$^&%$." Along with this cursing, the only intelligible words we could understand were "the well," "stupid horse" and "get the gun." It was a toss-up: should we get out of there as quickly as we could, or should we get closer and find out what was causing all the commotion?

We decided on the getting-closer option, and parked the half-ton with the other trucks. As we approached the well, we saw where the plank floor underneath the pump of the windmill had broken into bits.

Uncle Jake, or Unc, as I called him, stormed around the well, cursing and yelling at no one in particular. The rest of the crowd stood back at a respectful distance, not wanting to be part of Unc's wrath. The crane was positioned right over the well, and everyone hovered anxiously around it. They took no notice of us as we quietly approached and looked into the well.

We couldn't believe what we saw. Down in the well, wedged between its walls, was Queenie, Unc's prize Percheron mare. A man was precariously positioned on top of Queenie, trying to attach a rope around her belly. This was not an easy task, as Queenie had a very large, round belly, which was now squeezed to fit into the well. From the way she whinnied, we could tell that she was under a great deal of stress and very uncomfortable. It probably felt something like being squeezed into a girdle two sizes too small.

Eventually they hoisted Queenie up from her watery prison by means of the crane. The poor animal was weak and her lovely coat was scraped from being rubbed by the stones on the sides of the well. With wobbly legs she staggered tentatively around the yard, keeping her distance from the well. Unc regained his composure and when he saw his precious horse was still able to move, he stopped his cursing.

It took Queenie several months to recuperate, but she went on to establish herself as a top show horse and the pride of Unc's impressive stable of horses. B.J. was impressed with the entertainment that we provided for her first farm visit. She returned many times, but nothing equalled that initial exposure to the quiet life in the country.

Uncle Jake, thanks to Queenie and her imprisonment in the well, had one more, strange story to add to his repertoire. With each telling and as time passed, the well got deeper, the adventure grew more dangerous, and the story was always laced with Uncle Jake's colourful language!

CHAIRMAN OF THE BOARD

"THE ROLLANDS WON'T HAVE her!" The Chairman of the Board had spoken. The words were ominous and added another measure of panic to my already fear-laden heart. I was the new greenhorn teacher and no one wanted me. It couldn't be more obvious; the Chairman of the Board had spoken and he wielded a lot of power in the community. One of the first things I learned as a young teacher was not to question the Chairman of the Board.

The Chairman only came up to my nose, but the dignity with which he carried himself compensated for his lack of height, and his sense of self-importance seemed to add substance to his narrow shoulders. His voice was booming and authoritative. His piercing blue eyes were blazing and hypnotic and looked right into my inner being. They scared the life right out of this new teacher.

I was uncertain of my next move. I had travelled many miles in advance of the school year to rent a room locally, assuming that there would be a home in the community to take in the new teacher. But there it was in plain English. "The Rollands won't have her!" If not the Rollands, then who?

The Chairman continued to make phone calls to people within the community to see if someone would take me in. The more refusals he received, the more my spirits sagged. Perhaps the former teacher had been such a problem that no one wanted to risk taking the new one in? Another thought leaped into my mind. Maybe the school board had found something in my past which made me a bad risk. But how could this be? My only lawless act that I could recall was getting a speeding ticket. Surely that wasn't a serious enough infraction to cause all this delay.

In the midst of all this turmoil, the Chairman's three young children were acting up and showing off for their new teacher. I tried to treat them with love and patience, but all I could really focus on was the fact that no one wanted me—panic had started to set in.

To add to the chaos, every time one of the kids acted up, the Chairman said in a threatening voice, "Behave yourselves, or the teacher will give you a skite!" I wasn't quite sure what a "skite" was, but was reasonably certain that it was something I wouldn't think of giving to a young child.

Finally, after a particularly long phone conversation that involved a bit of grumbling on the Chairman's part, he faced me with a smile of relief on his small, wrinkled face. "Ernie and Ruth will have you." What sweet words to my ears!

The Chairman directed me to their place, where I found a charming couple that didn't appear too eager to "have me," but agreed to a trial run until Christmas. From that moment on, it was like being on double parole. Not only did I have to prove myself at teaching, I also had to pass muster at the house where I was boarding.

It was a lot of pressure on a young girl who didn't have the faintest idea what she was going to do in the classroom. I had spent only six weeks in Toronto at summer school learning everything I needed to know about running a classroom. I was a true novice. My audacity was tempered by the thought of teaching students only a few years my junior. It was a scary thought!

Ernie and his wife Ruth empathized with me and recognized that I was really just a kid that needed some mothering. However, a red flag went up when Ruth hugged me and said, "Don't listen to all the things they tell you about the kids in the school. You'll get along just fine, I'm sure!" No one had told me, the 18-year-old greenhorn with only six weeks of training, anything about the kids in this school. But it sounded ominous.

I returned to the Chairman's house and timidly requested a set of school keys. He didn't seem to have much confidence in me, for he questioned the fact that

I needed my own set of keys. I explained that if I had my own keys, I would not have to bother him so much. That fact appealed to him and he relented.

I drove into the school yard and sat in the car trying to build up enough bravado to enter the building. This was my school and my yard. It was a sobering thought. After a quarter of an hour passed, I gulped, stopped my knees from shaking, and got out of the car. I walked around the playground pretending to inspect it, but in reality, I was slowly trying to drum up courage. Then I saw a little building tucked away in the corner of the yard behind some brush.

Oh no! It couldn't be! Surely not! I approached the building and about ten feet away from it my suspicions were confirmed. It was indeed "the dreaded outdoor toilet." I had laughed at stories my father had told about his school years when he and his friends tipped the outhouse with the teacher in it. Right then and there I vowed never to use the facilities until all the school children went home for the day. And I was true to that vow. I conditioned myself to use the facilities only at 4:30 p.m. Not once during the school year did I venture near the outhouse until the coast was clear.

Using my own private, personal set of keys, I entered the school and took in the atmosphere of the one-room classroom that would be mine for the next year. I practised what I would say the first morning and tried to stand tall. I decided that standing behind the desk was a good move—then the 36 students wouldn't see my shaking knees.

During the first three days of my teaching career I had trouble maintaining order. The students were, no doubt, testing me. Some of them were only a couple of years younger than me and did their best to rattle me. In an effort to establish control and assert authority, I frequently pounded on the floor with a yardstick. They weren't the sturdiest yardsticks and they often broke.

In that era of teaching all the school supplies had to be approved by the Chairman of the Board. Knocking on the Chairman's door to request a new yardstick three days in a row was embarrassing, so I found another tactic that worked even better.

I was young, but not dumb. I reasoned that if the Chairman of the Board instilled fear in me, he was probably an awesome figure to the students as well. The next day, after this illumination, I wrote on the blackboard, THE CHAIRMAN OF THE BOARD, and underlined the words. I explained that the next one to disobey or cause trouble would have their name written below his title and be dealt with by the Chairman himself. It worked. No one wanted to tangle with him.

The rest of year was challenging, but there were no more discipline problems and no more yardstick replacements. Ernie and Ruth, the people I boarded with, were good to me and treated me like the daughter they never had. They agreed to keep me the whole school year and even tried to arrange my social life by inviting young eligible bachelors of the neighbourhood in for visits.

I continued to teach for 30 more years, but no one ever left such a lasting first impression on me as the Chairman of my first school board.

WOODMAN SPARE THAT TREE

THE BIG OLD MAPLE TREE in the corner of the school yard was a dear friend. In the hot June days we had story time under its long shady branches.

When the maple tree shed its keys, we gathered them up in piles, climbed up on the highest part of the play structure and flung them down to the ground. They became whirling, twirling miniature helicopters right before our eyes, and we raced to see whose would land first. In the fall it became a mass of red leaves—leaves that were raked up and used as a jumping target. Winter found the tree bare and stark-looking. However, on those dreaded ice storm days, it became a thing of beauty with its silver branches sparkling in the sun. We watched faithfully for the first sign of buds in the springtime and for the foliage to reappear. The tree was our harbinger of the seasons and a wonderful teaching aid.

But one day, disaster struck.

During a severe thunderstorm our tree was hit by lightning and was almost split into two pieces. The "administration," from their remote ivory towers, immediately dispatched a tree-cutting crew to clean up the broken branches and cut down the wounded maple. The cherry picker machine arrived on the scene and soon a brave man was in its basket, ready to do whatever has to be done to fallen trees.

I couldn't see our dear friend tree disappear without an effort to save it, so I ran out into the yard with the children following. I flung myself in front of the tree and begged them not to cut it down. After regaining my composure somewhat, I asked them if there wasn't some way to save the maple. I drew upon all the logical reasons why the tree should stay. Most important, I explained, the tree was a crucial part of our playground.

I could see that they didn't quite know how to deal with the situation and I'm sure they questioned my sanity. The principal was alerted to the situation and appeared on the scene. I told him my story first. Before long there were discussions on alternative ways of dealing with the wounded tree. It was hard enough on the neck to look up at a man in a cherry picker for an extended period of time, but even more difficult to carry on an intelligent and rational discussion with someone who was about to cut down a beautiful old tree, one that carried so many memories. We finally convinced him to come down from his lofty post, and then, slowly and systematically, we sorted out the problem.

The final decision was to give the tree a fighting chance to heal and recover from the storm trauma. Even with their help, the crew figured the tree would only live a year or two, but they came back the next day to do some repairs. They wrapped a big cable around the split and drew the two sections of the tree together. They also sealed the wound with a black oily tar mixture.

That was about 20 years ago, and the beautiful maple still stands in all its grandeur in the corner of the playground. It offers shade to all who settle under its full-branched crown. It sends its keys to those who would make helicopters. It foretells the seasons to all who care to see. And if you look away up into its branches you can still see the cable and the black tar.

Sometimes it's important to take a stand!

STU AND HIS TRUCKS

STU IS MY HUSBAND, and for me he is the perfect 10 in most areas. However, his trucks are the bane of my existence. Stu delivers shavings with a small fleet of five trucks. All of them are in various states of disrepair. He loads the trucks with shavings from different planing mills and then delivers them to horse and dairy farmers for bedding. This means that he is on the road a great deal. And since time passes more quickly with company, there are always two or three of his good buddies who are ready to endure the hardships of driving with him in exchange for his company and conversation.

Not only are the cabs dusty from the shavings, but the heaters seldom put out enough warmth to keep the windshields clear in the winter. None of the doors and windows close securely and, as one might suspect, the exhaust systems are not state of the art. But the cab has ambience—holes are covered with a spray sealant that looks like shaving cream foam, creating a spaceship-like atmosphere.

When it comes to repairs, well, procrastination is one of Stu's greatest assets. An asset because he has an easy-going philosophy about life. "Doesn't do much good to get riled up!" he would say. Stu would never suffer from an ulcer, even though the people around him might!

The Department of Transport inspectors know Stu well. They often conduct spot checks on his vehicles to see what part is about to fall off next. Getting pulled off the road by the Ministry for some infraction doesn't get Stu upset. It's just part of the day's work. He merely calls home on his cell phone to be rescued. He and his buddy of the day simply sit, chat and wait until help comes. He always carries his cell phone, but seldom turns it on— that way, no one can contact him, but he has it for his emergencies. At times it's difficult to deal with his "confounded contentedness."

Al is one of Stu's best friends and endures many truck trips in vehicles that often defy description. Take the rainy-day adventure they shared.

Al kept moving closer and closer to Stu in his five-ton Ford truck. It wasn't until they were almost touching elbows that Stu even noticed. It simply took all of Stu's efforts and attention to keep the old '77 truck on the road without worrying about his passenger! And poor Al was only trying to avoid the rain splatters that had started to soak him on the passenger side.

Finally Stu realized that Al was almost in his lap. "Is there a problem, Al?" he asked.

"Not now," replied Al. "The rain was coming in through a hole in the floor boards next to my door. But I'm okay now, and I guess I'll dry out. I'm not sugar or salt so I'll be fine!" Al held up his pant legs, which were soaked from the knee down.

"Huh! Guess I'll have to fix that hole someday," was Stu's only reply.

And he was right. The big gaping hole in the floor of the '77 Ford truck needed immediate attention. Since it didn't directly impact on Stu, there was no urgency to the problem. Furthermore, it wasn't a problem on dry days, so he just plain forgot about it until the next time it rained and a passenger got wet.

Then there were the windshield and the windshield wipers to deal with. On rainy days like this when the road is difficult to see, Stu had to deal with the accumulated layers of dusty grime on the windshield. Since there was never any wiper fluid, the dirt build-up was considerable. In fact, it was only recently that the old truck had a complete windshield at all! As well, Stu often had to struggle with the wipers—just getting them into position so they would work was a task. In Stu's mind, these were just other parts of his vehicle that needed fixing. I can only assume that the pleasure of Stu's company far outweighed the minor inconveniences that every passenger was familiar with.

I accompanied him once, and only once. It was his birthday and none of his buddies could go with him, so I felt a certain responsibility. I swallowed my pride and decided to keep him company on his special day.

It was no small feat for me to even board the truck. It was high off the ground and I was not! After what amounted to a running, flying leap I finally managed to get one cheek on the seat. Stu tugged at me from the driver's side until I fell awkwardly face down on the dusty seat. I clawed and wiggled—finally my whole body was inside the cab. Stu reached across to close my door. I was imprisoned for the next four hours.

I regained some sense of decorum and tried to make small talk. Competing with the noise of the engine and the muffler system that emitted a horrible roar every time he accelerated didn't make it easy. So much for conversing. I decided to tidy up the cab. In spite of the awesome task, I was undaunted. I collected all the empty pop cans and stashed them into an old greasy bag; the McDonald's garbage was put into another greasy bag to recycle. A collection of repair bills and receipts was put into the glove compartment—that pretty well cleared off the dashboard. One old dusty letter remained lying face down on the dash. To my horror, I discovered it to be an important letter I had given Stu to mail about two months previously. We exchanged "words," above the noises of the truck. To his advantage, he could barely hear what I was saying. I tried to remain calm. After all, it was his birthday.

Since the passenger door didn't close tightly, it was both drafty and cool, so I turned on the heater.

What a mistake that was! The accumulated dust and shavings in the air vents blew all over the cab and reduced us both to fits of coughing and sputtering.

Stu very kindly stopped at the next truck stop, and got me a drink to soothe my throat. I sipped slowly at the canned drink, resting it at my feet in between sips—there was no room for it on the front seat beside us. At the very last gulp, I felt something on my lips and I let out a scream that even overpowered the engine of the truck. A wasp had settled in the can and with the next gulp it had landed on my lips. Fortunately, I wasn't stung.

When we arrived home, my eagerness to disembark made it much easier and more expedient to exit the truck than my earlier attempt at boarding. Stu thanked me for spending his birthday with him, but neither one of us ever suggested that I go again.

Stu continues to truck and welcomes any companion who dares to make the trip with him. Sonny, Al and Joe are regulars, and have much the same philosophy as Stu. Life problems are dealt with, politics discussed, farming practices compared, get-rich-quick schemes tossed around and local gossip exchanged. The one criterion for trucking with Stu is to be free of time constraints, and it helps to share his philosophy of not getting riled up. When you drive with Stu, you can always count on either a mechanical breakdown or a major hold-up by the Department of Transport inspectors. Sharing his philosophy of "confounded contentedness" goes a long way when you're riding with Stu.

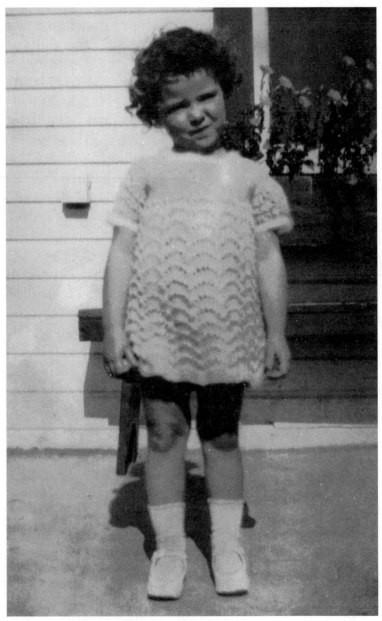

THE AUTHOR AT AGE 4

ABOUT THE AUTHOR

MOST OF THE STORIES in this collection, *Rural Reflections,* are drawn from distant memories of growing up in Lanark County and a few more recent recollections of my life as a teacher and wife.

I was the youngest of four children born to Isabel and Thom McGill of Pakenham. My Mother was an "a" Isabel and I was an "o" Isobel. It was because my parents had such streaks of individuality that my growing up years were so interesting. We lived on the homestead farm doing mixed farming. In the 1940s Dad began raising mink, foxes and chinchillas until the bottom fell out of the fur market. My father declared that it was difficult to have a livelihood that depended on the whims of women. As a result, we expanded the dairy side of the operation, which, according to Dad, still involved temperamental females.

I attended a one-room schoolhouse and learned to love literature at an early age. I can recall one teacher reading us the book, *Cue for Treason,* and I thought it was the best story I had ever heard. That started a love affair with books that continues today. I went to High School in Almonte and then became a teacher. After three years of teaching, I married the love of my life, Stu, and together we raised four wonderful children. After a ten-year absence from teaching I returned to the classroom. It was an eventful return. The school burned down on the second day of classes! I taught at North Gower Marlborough Public School for the next twenty-seven years and received a degree in

Psychology from Carleton University through night classes and summer courses. After thirty years in the classroom, I retired and found the time and energy to do some writing.

The first book I wrote was a collection of humourous things the children in my Kindergarten classes said over the years. It is entitled *Out of the Mouths of Babes* and has sold well. The second book was a children's story called *When We Were Just Born*. It has also been a successful venture. With these two books, I have enjoyed doing many presentations with primary school children in different schools.

Writing this third book, *Rural Reflections,* has taken me down memory lane. I hope you will enjoy the journey as you are introduced to characters and events from my life of "growing up rural in Lanark County."